30 L(esson)s Under 30

On How to Be A Person: A Reflection on Trial and Error

Jamie Ehrenfeld

30 L(esson)s Under 30 On How to Be A Person: A Reflection on Trial and Error © 2022 Jamie Ehrenfeld

Presentation by *BookLeaf Publishing*

Web: www.bookleafpub.com

E-mail: info@bookleafpub.com

ISBN: 9789395756372

First edition 2022

DEDICATION

For my family, my community, and all my
fellow compliment-deflectors out there

PREFACE

This book's existence is the fulfillment of a promise I made to myself: to let myself be seen artistically, imperfections and all. As this publication aligns with the passing of my thirtieth solar return, I affirm, however quietly, that my creative work is worthy of taking up space. I hold hope that these words may make you feel seen, too.

Scrambled Poetry

I've always said I have
too many words for poetry
tumbling too quickly
in through me and out
ideas diverging
synapses on fire
and then all of a sudden
it's lights out

I've forgotten where I am
and the point of it all
So I make a life raft of words
with too many words
moving too fast
in coherent but not cohesive
thoughts
fueled by strong but not long
feelings
that I skirt with my words
for safety
circling around the pressure points
in hopes I can make them hurt less
do less of what they do
and more of just
explaining
why

I cannot simply breathe, slow and steady
and hold onto them all
while I prepare and serve up
a hot plate of
scrambled poetry.

Submersion

Descent into lower frequency
Submerges me into slow motion
Depth led paralysis
Confronted with the truth of
Past present but not
future if I hold steady to
the journey through the storm
rather than around it
there's only one way
we make it out of here
alive.

Depression
is it a black hole
entropy or inertia?
the heaviness of
grinding steel to a
screeching halt
stubbornly staid
aching from root
chakra to crown
gravity from within
poised for total collapse
painstakingly slowly
an existential exhaustion.

and some days
the depression wins.

I grieve every loss like it's you

The love I see in the mirror
Eyes of someone close
bringing me alive like new
Like you
Arrived in the lessons I needed
In the vessels that could deliver them
Hitting me with the pull of
true love tangled in codependency
We occupied me and I still couldn't see
that every loss in this life is not
you

Ripping me open each time
A little wider, cutting scars out
from deeper than I could see before
but the thought of letting go
pulled me right back to
how every time, I feel
you
Or rather, your shadow
rising through
every loss that holds meaning
wrapped in the deepest grief
Until I let go of
every loss being
you.

Age

The passage of days on its own does not age us
Not like the tough life lessons of
growing up that can happen anytime
Without warning, at any time
life may show you
what hell adulthood can bring

I am an emotional Benjamin Button
Never younger or more carefree
Light after a long night snuggling life's ugly
underside
Because I've seen too much too soon
Three year olds shouldn't know how the movie
ends just yet

Art

is the transference
of spiritually connected consciousness
into life among us on earth
embodied and manifested
through heroes that thankfully
didn't listen
when they were told
to get a real job.

30 L's Under 30 (part 1)

What I have lost
must be honored as past tense
even if I'm still making it so

What I have lost
is the need to hold onto
everyone I've ever loved
is the compulsion to fix everyone else
when I'm the one in most need of attention
is my resentment toward the concept of
deserving

What I have lost
is the desire to serve at my own peril
is the delusion that the right work
will be enough alone to fulfill me
is the resistance to feeling the things
work helped me to avoid feeling

What I have lost
is the idea that I am an object
upon which life simply occurs
is the obsession with figuring out
how this all ends
is the insistence that I can

think my way out of emotional pain
without letting it be seen and felt
acknowledged

What I have lost
is the urge to rush myself
is the resistance to living in unknowns
is the weight of grief
constantly sat upon my psyche

I take these L's and many more
but this time, the loss is welcome

Infinite, Binary Choices

This is a life of infinite binary choices.
Countless each day, distinct determinations
This, or that? Yes, or no? Stay or leave?
To choose is to affirm what is,
by asserting what is not.
When we choose truly
we claim what we honestly want
submitting the uncomfortable truth to the
universe
to do with it what it will

like it doesn't already know
like it's not the one electrifying nerve endings
snaking through guts, around hearts
like it doesn't understand how hard it is
in our environments
full of multiplicities
to make choices in alignment with ourselves
truly
but in recognizing us doing our part
preparations have already begun

we are where we are
existing as we do
in relationship with our surroundings

and communities
making infinite, binary choices
this, or that?

where are you going?

Learning

to be light
even if just a warm glow
here to take the edge off
when it's all too much to take

Maybe

If I sink into myself
and simmer long enough
I'll rise whole.

Maybe
If I pack light enough
I can float into the atmosphere
Before becoming a part of it

Maybe
Screams of possibility without security
Calls for faith with no certainty

Maybe
The lightest and heaviest word
Holding hope and despair in equal measure

Maybe
purgatory in a word
suspended in mid air
dualities unknown

Maybe
Someday I'll release need to decipher

what's hidden beneath my maybes

Maybe.

Water

I pray to the ocean
constant flowing
cascading waves
crashing into land but for a brief moment
until gracefully retreating into its source
just more before blessing us
with a new wave
unique and of one simultaneously

full of life
multitudes and ecosystems
sustaining themselves with loving balance
gentle, yet deadly
humble, often calm
yet unquestionably more powerful
than we are
occupying its space
inviting us to enjoy the ride
if you dare
teaching faith and vigilance
all at once

You Taught Me

To go where the love is
from both sides of the lesson

I heard you right the first time
but this last time got me twisted
clinging ghosts and shadows
tempted once again to
run this train right into the ground
at least then I'll know we're past saving
because as sad as it is
for so long just a glimmer
was enough hope to hold me

Hatred of Self

Did you always hate seeing yourself?
Was it once you felt time had betrayed you
Or when you heard the world say that
your natural existence was wrong?

The contingence of worthiness to be seen
on external expectations
upholding toxic powers
slowly but surely
buried you
and many others
pointing blame inward
like this experience
is the source of the problem

Pain is not equally distributed
Forcing someone to face
the excruciating nature of
enduring societal violence
While those inflicting it
aren't required to do the same
is not fair, nor will it lead to nirvana

how can we truly reckon
with ourselves and with each other
without individually
and collectively crumbling?

Little Girl in the Pink Dress

Dancing at her daddy's funeral
Lifting moods since she was still light
Grief hadn't sunk in because
Young children live in holistic absolutes

Over time I steeped in loss like a strong tea
In a culture where this is what happens
and isn't it always the tragedy
a curse
Defining moment over moment like there's
moments to spare
When we know all too well that there aren't

I don't wear pink dresses anymore
they feel much too heavy
holding expectations of childlike joy and wonder
I haven't known well since that day

Children's job is to be the light, as they are
Adult's job is to let the light in
and share lessons learned from the dark
not to scare us
but to arm us as we grow

I traded my pink dress for armor
that I'm learning now to lay down

Judge, Jury and Executioner

"Mental illnesses
are excuses for people that can't handle things
are day-passes for dysfunction
are things only the weak must endure

Can't you control yourself?
What's
wrong
with
you?"

I faked it with the best of them
Not noticing myself or surroundings
Took twenty-five to see it
And another five to let go
When the lens itself
obscured my vision
Framing what and how I know
Reality a subjectively tricky bitch
Where rights and wrongs
do and do not exist
based on context

Trap Door

After trauma, triggers set like trap doors
ready to drop you back down to
the moment that wrecked you
suddenly as safe
as you were then
which is to say--
not.

The climb back up is more exhausting each time
Feeling familiar, like a curse that echoes
Ripple effects rolling in
No notice, no warning
Like your nightmare's on a constant loop and
it's already come true.

The Nature of Truth

Truth in our society is
underlaid with objectivism
Science
Pics or it didn't happen
Evidence
Facts proven through
careful experimentation
methodology bound by
proper protocol
due diligence
and data

Data
information
bits of truth telling
record keeping
meticulous documentation
but where is the soul of the truth?
in us, as we are
in egos set on proving
superiority or rightness
in tribalist defenders
tearing down the other
because truth is often determined

on a deeper level
in a realer sense
by might

Love

is the
baseline
and also
the bassline

Bumps with each beat
Holds you down in all the best ways
Presence felt more than spoken
Nestled in foundation of a much grander plan
Its absence brings a sense of empty
That perhaps you can't quite place

Love is
the
baseline
and also
the bassline.

Music is

inherently sensual
vibrations buzz in light
molecules bouncing
up and down
putting on all kinds of a show
dictating the way and time in which we move
rhythms colliding to form
a soundscape of
wonder
nostalgia
imaginary getaway
or just the soundtrack to our lives
penetrating any and all of our
resistance to feeling.

Do you ever

just stop
look around
and recognize
the unfolding
of your life itself
as art?

30 Lessons Under 30 (part 2)

Beyond a life of losses
I have learned.

I have learned
that nothing and everything is personal
that the laws of momentum and inertia apply to
us too
that we all do need someone, but no one needs
everyone

I have learned
that everybody has mommy / daddy issues
even when their issues
aren't issues
like mine

I have learned
that most often, we break our own hearts
when the pain starts to feel like home
until we face the music of our deepest wounds
we keep the beat on ourselves
violently and subversively

I have learned that
you cannot control others

without enacting abuse
and the mental
emotional kind counts too

I have learned
that money's only real when you don't have it
that credit's a game they hope you don't know
how to play
and that we're already all on borrowed time

I have learned
that we each have our own calculus
of priorities guiding choices
with the weight of factors based on
proximity to heartstrings pulling at
sources of trauma and fear
and our values

most importantly, I have learned
that freedom comes in understanding
I have limits. I have powers.
and what's beyond me is beyond me
but I can do things
even when it feels like
nothing matters
and I've got me
more than I've ever
had me before

Don't

overwater
the
plants

to know what's enough
and what is too much
is the superpower of
care and attention
paired with release
and trust in the universe
that your efforts are seen
and you've done your best
even when that means
nothing but waiting now